Presented to

by

on

A CHILD'S FIRST BIBLE

PSALMS

for Little Hearts

written by Dandi Daley Mackall | illustrated by Cee Biscoe

Tyndale House Publishers, Inc.
Carol Stream, Illinois

For Harper Nora Mackall, with love and a prayer that the Psalms will help you through life

Visit Tyndale's website for kids at www.tyndale.com/kids.

Visit Dandi Daley Mackall online at www.dandibooks.com.

A Child's First Bible: Psalms for Little Hearts

Designed by Libby Dykstra (special thanks to Ruth Pizzi)

Edited by Stephanie Rische

For manufacturing information regarding this product, please call 1-800-323-9400.

For information about special discounts for bulk purchases, please contact Tyndale House Publishers at csresponse@tyndale.com, or call 1-800-323-9400.

Library of Congress Cataloging-in-Publication Data
Names: Mackall, Dandi Daley, author.
Title: A child's first bible : psalms for little hearts / Dandi Daley Mackall.
Description: Carol Stream, Illinois : Tyndale House Publishers, [2019] |
Series: A child's first Bible | Audience: Ages 4-7.
Identifiers: LCCN 2018009778 | ISBN 9781496432759 (hc)
Subjects: LCSH: Bible. Psalms–Paraphrases, English–Juvenile literature. |
Children–Prayers and devotions–Juvenile literature. |
Children–Religious life–Juvenile literature.

Classification: LCC BS1440 .M327 2019 | DDC 223.2–dc23 LC record available at https://lccn.loc.gov/2018009778

Printed in China

25
7 6 5 4 3 2

Contents

Introduction

IS THE BOOK OF PSALMS STILL RELEVANT for today's kids? Do children really need to hear the ancient songs and poems? Of course! God never changes, and his Word still changes us. The psalmists spoke out of the depth of their emotions—loneliness, despair, guilt, confusion. They cried out to God for the same reasons we do. Their feelings are our feelings—and the feelings of our children. In a unique way, the Psalms can point us to God as the source of hope; the means of forgiveness; and the path to righteousness, wisdom, joy, and praise.

I have a special place in my heart for this book of the Bible. Every time I read a psalm, it's as if God has been reading my mail and listening in on my every thought. I want that to happen for each child who hears these psalms. This book is not a direct translation of the book of Psalms but an attempt to relate the spirit and meaning of each psalm in a way that children will grasp. My goal on these pages is to maintain the theme, the integrity, and certain wording of each psalm, and ultimately to make it easier for the heart of the psalmists to touch the heart and mind of a child.

You can use this book in any way that works for your family. You might want to read one psalm each night at bedtime, or you could incorporate a psalm into your family devotions. You can also consult the table of contents to help a child who's going through a particular problem—fear, loss, loneliness, sadness, or ingratitude—or to speak to a child who needs wisdom, direction, rest, forgiveness, or hope.

My prayer is that through these pages, your child will come to meet God in a new and profound way and that your child will grow in love—a lifelong love of the Psalms, a love of life, and a forever love of our God.

Dandi Daley Mackall

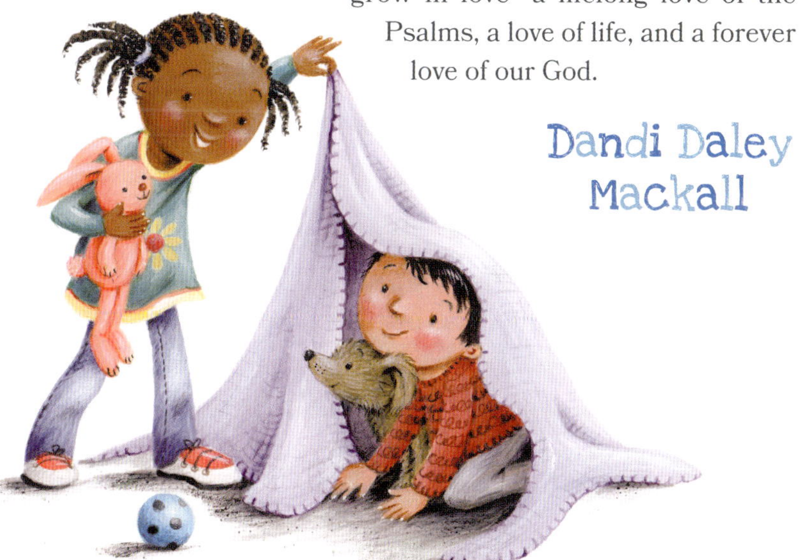

God Smiles at Me

A Psalm for When You Need Comfort

There's a kid who calls me names,
Leaves me out of fun and games.
I'm the one that big kid blames.
So, Lord, are you smiling at me?

I'm in trouble. I'm so mad!
Not *my* fault. I wasn't bad.
Take my anger. Make me glad.
Lord, won't you smile down on me?

But I'll come to you in prayer.
Nice to know you're always there.
Great to feel your loving care
And know you are smiling at me.

Thanks for Mom, and thanks for Dad;
They bring comfort when I'm sad.
Tell me, how could I feel bad
When you, Lord, are smiling at me?

Pouncing puppy licks my nose.
Muddy puddles, muddy toes.
See that robin? There it goes!
I know you are smiling at me.

Playing baseball? Count me in!
Shout out, "Let the games begin!"
If I lose, or if I win . . .
Well, you're still smiling at me.

Hip, hooray, the city zoo!
Who made zebras? I know who!
Good things always come from you.
Lord, you are smiling at me.

Silly monkeys, tall giraffes,
Hoot owl hoots, hyena laughs—
Taking funny photographs.
That's you still smiling at me.

Greeting people on the street,
Bringing joy to those I meet—
Thanks to you, life's pretty sweet!
For you are smiling at me.

Feel that laughter in the rain?
See my moon-striped windowpane?
In the distance . . . hear that train?
And you're still smiling at me.

Say my prayers and settle in,
Knowing you forgive my sin.
You're where all good things begin.
God, thanks for smiling at me!

Many people say,
"Who will show us better times?"
Let your face smile on us, LORD.
You have given me greater joy
than those who have abundant
harvests of grain and new wine.
In peace I will lie down and sleep,
for you alone, O LORD,
will keep me safe.

PSALM 4:6-8

God's Beautiful World

A Psalm of Praise

Every night sky is the work of your hands—
Billions of stars lighting God's wonderlands.
Planets and comets obey your commands.
Everything shows us your glory!

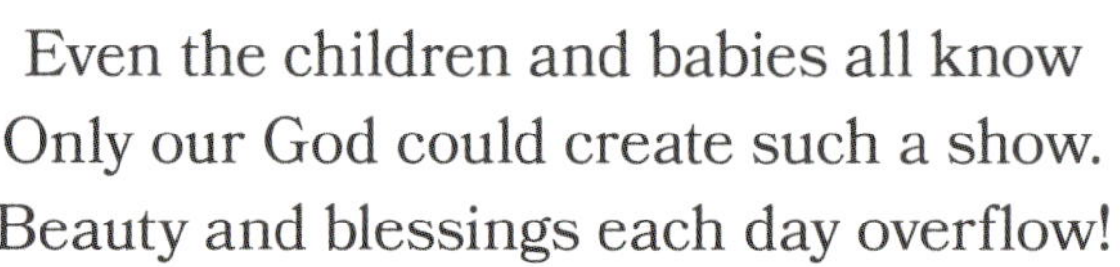

Even the children and babies all know
Only our God could create such a show.
Beauty and blessings each day overflow!
Everything shows us your glory.

Even your enemies have to admit
You made the heavens and earth, bit by bit.
Wow! Your creation's a super smash hit!
Everything shows us your glory.

Here's what I wonder—to me, it's unclear:
Why do you bother with people down here?
How can you care for us year after year?
Everything shows us your glory.

Lord, you have made us a part of your story,
Given us honor and crowned us with glory,
Told us to keep your world all hunky-dory.
Everything shows us your glory.

Now we're in charge of the skies and the seas,
Animals, fish, and the birds and the trees.
Help us, dear Lord, to be worthy trustees.
Everything shows us your glory!

O LORD, our Lord, your majestic name fills the earth!
Your glory is higher than the heavens. . . .
When I look at the night sky and see the work of your fingers—
the moon and the stars you set in place—
what are mere mortals that you should think about them,
human beings that you should care for them?
Yet you made them only a little lower than God
and crowned them with glory and honor.
You gave them charge of everything you made,
putting all things under their authority.

PSALM 8:1, 3-6

God Is My Rock

A Psalm for When You Are Afraid

I love you, Lord! You're my strength, my rock.
You can be my shepherd. And I'll be your flock.
If you built a tower, I would be a block.
O Lord, you're my strength, my rock!

You're my fortress, Lord. What's a fortress do?
Well, a fort protects and defends me too.
Then the best fort wins, and the best is YOU.
O Lord, you're my fortress, my rock!

Lord, you give me strength.
You're my sword and shield.
And you're by my side on the battlefield.
I will give three cheers when your plan's revealed.
O Lord, you're my strength and shield!

Only you, dear Lord, are my safety place.
Only you can calm with your saving grace.
How I long to talk with you face-to-face.
O Lord, you're my safety place!

You're my stronghold, Lord, when I wake at night.
If I feel afraid, then you hold me tight.
Let the darkness fall. You're my guiding light.
O Lord, you're my stronghold and light!

There's no other God. You're the one true king.
Your unfailing love touches everything.
Through eternity, we will praise and sing:
"O Lord, you're the one true king!"

Tell me, how on earth did you rescue me,
Reaching way down here just to set me free?
I'm as grateful, Lord, as a kid can be.
O Lord, you're my savior, my rock!

I could scale a wall or the monkey bars.
I could fly from Earth, maybe land on Mars.
I might catch a ride on some falling stars.
For you are my fortress, my rock!

I love you, LORD; you are my strength.
The LORD is my rock, my fortress,
and my savior; my God is my rock,
in whom I find protection.
He is my shield, the power that
saves me, and my place of safety.
I called on the LORD, who is worthy
of praise, and he saved me
from my enemies.

PSALM 18:1-3

Only God Could Do That!

A Psalm of Worship

Listen! Hear the heavens say,
"God is great in every way!"

Who else dares to touch the sky,
Shouting down from way up high?

Only God could make a cloud,
Soft and white . . . or gray and loud.

Late at night I sometimes wonder,
Who but God could make such thunder?

Our Creator formed the moon!
Listen—you can hear the tune.

Moonlit waters striped with light,
Glittering, skittering in the night.

Rise and shine to see the sun,
Bringing light to everyone.

Swimming, playing hide-and-seek,
Every week a Holy Week.

All God's laws are good and true,
Sweet as honey, through and through.

You created Promised Lands.
I will follow your commands.

Beauty right before my eyes!
Only you can make me wise.

Help my thoughts be kind and clear,
Full of love and free from fear.

Look around! Don't miss a thing!
Worship our Creator King!

Not a sound and not a word,
Still the voice of God is heard!

The heavens proclaim the glory of God.
The skies display his craftsmanship.
Day after day they continue to speak;
night after night they make him known.
They speak without a sound or word;
their voice is never heard.
Yet their message has gone
throughout the earth,
and their words to all the world.

PSALM 19:1-4

God Is My Shepherd

A Psalm for When You Need Protection

In valleys low or mountains steep,
You're my shepherd; I'm your sheep.

I've got everything I need.
I will follow. You can lead.

Pastures green and lakes so blue
Always make me think of you.

If I'm lost one stormy day,
You will help me find my way.

If I'm in a strange new place,
I can ask for peace and grace.

If a bully threatens me,
I'll be brave as brave can be.

I am weak, but you are strong.
I will praise you all day long.

You protect me—there's no doubt!
Trust is what it's all about.

Time to time, I need a rest.
Living in your house is best.

When I'm scared, you take my hand,
Keep me safe, and understand.

Mercy, love, and goodness, too—
All are mine because of you.

You're my shepherd all my days.
You deserve eternal praise!

The LORD is my shepherd;
I have all that I need.
He lets me rest in green meadows;
he leads me beside peaceful streams.
He renews my strength.
He guides me along right paths,
bringing honor to his name.
Even when I walk
through the darkest valley,
I will not be afraid,
for you are close beside me.
Your rod and your staff
protect and comfort me.

PSALM 23:1-4

God Gives Me Joy

A Psalm for When You Feel Sad

I pinched my sister. Then I lied.
I felt so guilty deep inside.
But you forgave me! You're my guide
To joy, joy, joy in my heart!

I goofed around when I got bored
And broke a plate my mom adored.
I took my problem to my Lord.
There's joy, joy, joy in my heart.

Today I broke the Golden Rule.
I lost the game and lost my cool.
I know I'm stubborn as a mule.
No joy, joy, joy in my heart.

When I admit my crummy sin,
It doesn't matter if I win.
My happiness will all begin
With joy, joy, joy in my heart.

So I confessed my sin to you.
I felt forgiveness through and through.
And now I start each day brand new
With joy, joy, joy in my heart!

Now you're my light, and you're my guide.
Please keep me walking by your side.
Then I will feel it deep and wide:
That joy, joy, joy in my heart.

I thank you, God, for love and grace.
You'll always be my hiding place.
In heaven, when we're face-to-face,
What joy, joy, joy in my heart!

Oh, what joy for those
whose disobedience is forgiven,
whose sin is put out of sight!
Yes, what joy for those
whose record the LORD has cleared
of guilt, whose lives are lived
in complete honesty! . . .
Many sorrows come to the wicked,
but unfailing love surrounds
those who trust the LORD.
So rejoice in the LORD and be glad,
all you who obey him! Shout for joy,
all you whose hearts are pure!

PSALM 32:1-2, 10-11

Taste and See

A Psalm for Trying New Things

I didn't like honey. I thought it looked icky.
So why should I try it and get my hands sticky?
But honey is sweet! I was just being picky.
So I had to taste and see.

I thought I'd hate spinach. Who wants to eat green?
The weirdest green veggie that I'd ever seen.
I tried it. I liked it! And here's what I mean . . .
I just had to taste and see.

I didn't like biking till I got a bike.
I thought walks were silly till I took a hike.
You never can tell what you're going to like . . .
Until you can taste and see.

I thought God was angry and totally scary.
I thought that this God stuff was not necessary.
And even in church I remained very wary.
I needed to taste and see.

Alone and so scared, my heart filled up with fear.
"Dear God, will you help me?
Dear God, are you here?"
Then I felt God answer. I knew he was near!
I just had to taste and see.

You think that it's hopeless? Please give God a try.
You don't have to go far. He's always nearby.
And trusting in God is as easy as pie!
You just have to taste and see.

Let's shout out God's goodness and celebrate grace!
We'll call on God's name anytime, anyplace.
And one day we'll talk with our Lord face-to-face.
We just have to taste and see.

Taste and see that the LORD is good.
Oh, the joys of those who take refuge in him! . . .
The eyes of the LORD watch over those who do right;
his ears are open to their cries for help.

PSALM 34:8, 15

God Fights for Me!

A Psalm for When You're the Underdog

I wish that I knew why they're picking on me.
Whatever I say, they will all disagree.
I lose every fight. They just won't let me be.
Lord, will you fight for me?

At lunch, I'm left out. So I eat on my own.
I fall and get hurt. They just laugh while I groan.
There's one thing I know: I can't fix this alone.
Lord, will you fight for me?

I'm scared to play ball 'cause I'm sure to strike out.
The minute I do, "You're a loser!" they shout.
So why do they blame me? What's that all about?
Lord, will you fight for me?

I did them no wrong. But they stay on the chase.
They dig me a trap so I'll fall on my face.
I wish THEY'D fall in, like they've fallen from grace.
Lord, will you fight for me?

She cheats on a test, but it's me that they blame.
Please bring out the truth so the cheater feels shame.
The next time it happens, I'll call on your name.
Lord, will you fight for me?

When they're sick, I feel sorry, the way that I should.
When I'm sick, they just laugh. I'm so misunderstood!
How I wish they'd quit giving me evil for good.
Lord, will you fight for me?

I'm begging for help, Lord. It just isn't fair!
I know that you're watching. I know that you're there.
I'm asking for justice. I know that you care.
Lord, will you fight for me?

I'll share your salvation and trust in your ways.
I'll shout of your greatness and sing out your praise!
I'll call to you faithfully all of my days.
Thank you for fighting for me!

*O Lord, oppose those who oppose me.
Fight those who fight against me. . . .
How long, O Lord, will you
look on and do nothing?
Rescue me from their fierce attacks.
Protect my life from these lions!
Then I will thank you in front
of the great assembly.
I will praise you before all the people.*

PSALM 35:1, 17-18

Trust in God

A Psalm for When You Don't Know What to Do

There are many days when I feel left out.
And it seems unfair, so I start to doubt.
Will you help me know what it's all about?
Then I'll trust in you and do good.

If a friend of mine has a bike that's new,
I might envy that 'cause I'd like one too.
Though I want that bike, I delight in you.
I will trust in you and do good.

When I lose a race that a bully wins,
Help me be okay, even if he sins.
You're the one who counts. That's where faith begins,
When I trust in you and do good.

I admit, at times it's so hard to wait.
But I'll trust in you—and you're never late!
'Cause with you in charge, things will be just great!
So I'll trust in you and do good.

Should I take this path? Should I make that choice?
Somewhere deep inside is a still, small voice.
Choosing God's way first makes my heart rejoice
When I trust in God and do good!

You will keep me safe as I grow and grow.
If the walls fall down, like in Jericho,
I will still march on, for by now I know:
I will trust in God and do good.

Everything I do, everywhere I go,
If I'm at a park or a rodeo,
If I'm sitting down or on tippy-toe,
I will trust in God and do good.

What the future holds, from my point of view,
Is a wondrous world where my dreams come true.
How can I be sure? Well, my hope's in you!
I will trust in you and do good.

*Trust in the LORD and do good.
Then you will live safely in
the land and prosper.
Take delight in the LORD,
and he will give you
your heart's desires.*
PSALM 37:3-4

God Rescues Me

A Psalm for When You're Sorry

I'm stuck deep in trouble as thick as the mud,
And problems come over me just like a flood.

I know I'm to blame as my sins pile up high,
Too many to count 'cause they reach to the sky.

So quickly, dear God! Will you rescue me, please?
I'm helpless before you and down on my knees.

I sure don't deserve it, but you're always near.
You're watching me, ready to wipe every tear.

I'm sad and I'm needy and scared as can be.
But could it be true that you're thinking of ME?

Please speak to me, Lord, and I'll listen—all ears.
'Cause your tender mercies can burst
through my tears!

Your blessings are mine, and there's nothing I lack.
And I know that you know I can't pay you back.

You loved and protected me, right from the start.
Thanks for instructions you write on my heart.

People who search for you find you are there,
Offering mercy and unending care.

Joy comes from you, Lord—I'll tell all my friends
News of salvation; your love never ends!

Lord, don't hold back your tender mercies from me.
Let your unfailing love and faithfulness always protect me.
For troubles surround me—
too many to count!
My sins pile up so high
I can't see my way out. . . .
But may all who search for you
be filled with joy and gladness in you.

PSALM 40:11-12, 16

I Long for God

A Psalm for When You Need Joy

Dear God, something's missing. I think that it's you.
A sadness comes over me out of the blue.
I look all around and don't know what to do.
Lord, am I longing for you?

I feel like a deer that cannot find a drink.
I'm longing and lost, with my brain out of sync.
I try, but I can't tell my mind what to think.
Lord, am I longing for you?

Once I was filled with a bubbly joy,
Feeling so thankful for every toy.
Now I'm not joyful, and boy, oh boy,
Lord, am I longing for you?

I try to be happy. I end up a fake.
I can't get to sleep—I just lie there awake.
I can't take much more or my poor heart might break.
Lord, am I longing for you?

I'm feeling so lousy. I wish I knew why.
And sometimes it seems you're too high in the sky.
But could it be someday we'll see eye to eye?
Lord, I am longing for you.

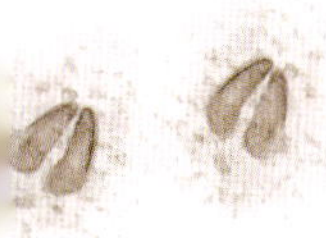

Give me a blue sky, and I'll turn it gray.
True, it's my fault if you feel far away.
I should remember to listen and pray.
Lord, I am longing for you.

Just when my sadness is bigger than me,
Dragging me down where I don't want to be—
That's when I'll turn and shout, "Lord, set me free!"
Lord, I am longing for you.

Even if all of the world says I'm wrong,
I will still praise you and sing you my song.
You pour your love on me all the day long.
That's why I'm longing for you!

As the deer longs for streams of water,
so I long for you, O God.
I thirst for God, the living God.
When can I go and stand before him? . . .
Why am I discouraged?
Why is my heart so sad?
I will put my hope in God!
I will praise him again—
my Savior and my God!

PSALM 42:1-2, 11

PSALM 46

Be Still

A Psalm for When You Need Peace

If an earthquake comes, and I feel it shake,
And my head and my heart and my feet all ache,
Though I want to run, there's too much at stake.
I'll be still and let God be God.

I get scared in fights. I don't want a war.
For the way to God is an open door.
When I long for peace, you will give me more.
I'll be still and let God be God.

It's a well-known fact: kingdoms come and go.
When their leaders brag, it is all for show.
But with God our King, blessings overflow!
So be still and let God be God.

I will follow God, even when I'm old.
When he takes my hand, I will grab ahold.
Then I'll walk with God on those streets of gold.
I'll be still and let God be God.

On that final day, at the trumpet call,
No one cares a bit if you're big or small.
For we'll bow our knees to the Lord of all
And be still and let God be God.

When we meet our God, we will be complete.
I can't wait to sit at my Master's feet!
In our heavenly home, it will be so sweet!
We'll be still and let God be God.

God is our refuge and strength,
always ready to help in times of trouble.
So we will not fear when earthquakes come
and the mountains crumble into the sea. . . .
"Be still, and know that I am God!
I will be honored by every nation.
I will be honored throughout the world."

PSALM 46:1-2, 10

I Love You More!

A Psalm of Love for God

I love you more than ninety-seven birthday cakes,
All the cookies Grandma bakes,
More than many recess breaks.

I love you more than blankies, bears,
and night-nights, too,
Sixty games of peekaboo,
Nineteen dreams that all come true.

I love you more than ninety rainbows in the sky,
Twenty blackbirds in a pie,
Fifteen falcons flying high.

I love you more than eighty-seven puppy dogs,
Tons and tons of chubby hogs,
Five-and-fifty croaking frogs.

I love you more than fifty-seven kitty cats,
Twenty billion birds and bats,
Half a trillion cowboy hats.

I love you more than fifty fish flip-flopping high,
Sixty bunnies, soft and shy,
Forty mules clip-clopping by.

I love you more than fourteen billion fancy cars,
Sun and moon and all the stars,
All the planets, even Mars!

I love you more than sixty million trillion toys,
Ninety girls and ninety boys,
Fireworks with all that noise.

I love you more than forty-seven butterflies,
Ten chameleons in disguise,
Twenty-seven lullabies.

I love you more than water on a summer's day.
You can take my thirst away!
You will hear me when I pray.

I love you more than all the snowflakes in the snow,
All of ME from head to toe!
I just wanted you to know . . . I still love you more.

You satisfy me more than the richest feast.
I will praise you with songs of joy.
I lie awake thinking of you,
meditating on you through the night.

PSALM 63:5-6

God Keeps Me Safe

A Psalm for When You Need Help

You are my hideout, my fortress, my rock.
You are our shepherd, and we are your flock.
You always open your door when I knock.
You'll always keep me safe.

Even before I was born on this earth,
You kept me safe. You were there at my birth.
You say that I have incredible worth.
You'll always keep me safe.

I can get scared on a Ferris wheel ride.
Noises and shadows and storms make me hide.
Nothing should scare me with you by my side.
You'll always keep me safe.

Save me and rescue me! You do what's right.
Please hear me calling you soft in the night.
You shine in shadows and show me the light.
You'll always keep me safe.

What if we're shopping and I end up lost—
Mommy and I get our signals all crossed?
You'll always find me, no matter the cost.
You'll always keep me safe.

If I'm alone, there's no cause for alarm.
I've never needed an old lucky charm.
I know you'll keep me from danger and harm.
You'll always keep me safe.

I can't stop praising you all the day long.
I'll shout your goodness and grace in a song.
Save me from evil, and keep me from wrong.
Thank you for keeping me safe.

I'll do my best to keep danger away.
I can be smart when I go out to play.
Deep in my heart, Lord, I just want to say:
Thank you for keeping me safe.

O Lord, I have come to you for protection;
don't let me be disgraced.
Save me and rescue me,
for you do what is right.
Turn your ear to listen to me,
and set me free.
Be my rock of safety
where I can always hide.
Give the order to save me,
for you are my rock and my fortress. . . .
O Lord, you alone are my hope.
I've trusted you, O Lord, from childhood.
Yes, you have been with me from birth;
from my mother's womb you have cared for me.
No wonder I am always praising you!

PSALM 71:1-3, 5-6

God Looks Out for Me

A Psalm for When You Need Rest

God is my shelter, and I need a rest.
Life is too crazy, so here's my request:
Father, protect me, for you do it best.
That's why my trust is in God.

Rescue me, Father, when I'm far away.
Keep me from those who would lead me astray.
I need you with me by night and by day.
That's why my trust is in God.

Hide-and-go-seek is my favorite game.
Hiding in you, Lord—it's not quite the same.
You always find me. I trust in your name.
That's why my trust is in God.

Even at night I have nothing to fear.
You will protect me, and you're always near,
Whispering promises only I hear.
That's why my trust is in God.

What if my bike cruises faster and faster?
What if a storm comes, and with it disaster?
I'll reach for God and hold hands with my Master.
That's 'cause my trust is in God.

I have some angels who watch over me,
If I'm on the shore or down under the sea.
Angels stand guard, so I live worry free!
That's why my trust is in God.

I'll look both ways before crossing the street,
Buckle up tight in my child-safety seat,
I'll be real careful, but let me repeat:
All of my trust is in God!

Those who live in the shelter of the Most High
will find rest in the shadow of the Almighty.
This I declare about the Lord:
He alone is my refuge, my place of safety;
he is my God, and I trust him. . . .
For he will order his angels
to protect you wherever you go.
They will hold you up with their hands
so you won't even hurt your foot on a stone.

PSALM 91:1-2, 11-12

Give Thanks

A Psalm of Gratitude

It is good to give thanks to the Lord,
To our God, who is loved and adored.

If I've nothing to do and I'm bored,
I can always give thanks to the Lord.

It is good, in the morning, to pray.
What a great way to start out the day—
Shouting thanks to the Lord, come what may.
It is good to give thanks to the Lord.

Then at night, oh, how faithful you are!
I can stare at the brilliant North Star
And rejoice in your works, near and far.
It is good to give thanks to the Lord.

I love cornfields and wheat fields and grass.
Thanks for all of the kids in my class.
In a test, thanks for helping me pass.

It is good to give thanks to the Lord.

When I'm feeling so weak or I'm sad,
When I try to be good but I'm bad,

When I don't get my way and I'm mad,
It is good to give thanks to the Lord.

How you thrill me with all that you do—
From my hat to the sole of my shoe!
I was born. Then I grew and I grew.
It is good to give thanks to the Lord.

I have friends and a family who care.
We have water and land and fresh air.
But the best gift is knowing you're there.
It is good to give thanks to the Lord.

Lord, you thrill me with all that you've done!
You're the King, the all-powerful one.
And your blessings have only begun!
It is good to give thanks to the Lord.

It is good to give thanks to the LORD,
to sing praises to the Most High.
It is good to proclaim your unfailing love
in the morning, your faithfulness in the evening,
accompanied by a ten-stringed instrument,
a harp, and the melody of a lyre.
You thrill me, LORD, with all
you have done for me!
I sing for joy because of what you have done.
O LORD, what great works you do!
And how deep are your thoughts.

PSALM 92:1-5

God Blesses Me

A Psalm for Counting Your Blessings

Counting my blessings is easy for me!
Look all around, and you'll see what I see.
Beautiful sights—and I think you'll agree:
Blessings are everywhere!

Sky that's so blue on a sunshiny day,
Clouds that make shapes and then up, up away!
Grass soft as silk in the field where we play.
Blessings are everywhere!

Sunrise and sunset, an everyday treat!
Daisies and roses and lilacs so sweet,
Dandelions, too—even they can't be beat!
Blessings are everywhere!

Moon shining bright in a star-studded sky,
Night disappears in the wink of an eye.
While we are sleeping, our gifts multiply!
Blessings are everywhere!

Cardinals and bluebirds tweet high in the trees,
Sending their songs on a soft summer breeze.
Robins and sparrows and sweet honeybees—
Blessings are everywhere!

Apples and oranges, bananas and pears,
Pink cotton candy at county-wide fairs,
Puppies and kittens and stallions and mares—
Blessings are everywhere!

Rain for the harvests of apples and wheat,
Bread on our table and good things to eat,
Mercies so tender—no trick, only treat.
Blessings are everywhere!

Mommies and daddies are blessings for sure.
Family and homes where we're safe and secure.
When we feel sick, you can send us a cure:
Blessings are everywhere!

I need forgiveness, and that comes from you.
You give us grace, like a dream that's come true,
Love that won't quit—every day it's brand new!
Blessings are everywhere!

Mercy from you, Lord, is better than best—
You move our sins far as east is from west.
I'll tell the world just how much I've been blessed!
Blessings are everywhere.

So many blessings that I cannot see.
Thanks for your Spirit, who's living in me.
Thanks for your blessings. They come to me free!
Blessings are everywhere.

Let all that I am praise the LORD;
with my whole heart, I will praise his holy name.
Let all that I am praise the LORD;
may I never forget the good things he does for me.
He forgives all my sins and heals all my diseases.
He redeems me from death and crowns me
with love and tender mercies.
He fills my life with good things.
My youth is renewed like the eagle's! . . .
The LORD is compassionate and merciful,
slow to get angry and filled with unfailing love. . . .
He has removed our sins as far from us
as the east is from the west.
The LORD is like a father to his children,
tender and compassionate to those who fear him.

PSALM 103:1-5, 8, 12-13

God Gives Me Wisdom

A Psalm for When You Need Direction

I'll give thanks to God for his wondrous deeds.
How he loves the poor! How he meets their needs!
I will follow God where my Savior leads.
And my God will give me wisdom.

I will think it out—it's the thing to do.
Then I'll look around, and I'll ponder who
Could create the birds and the cows that moo.
And my God will give me wisdom.

Let me hear good news and the old, old story,
For the Word reveals our Messiah's glory.
And the gifts God gives are just hunky-dory!
And my God will give me wisdom.

God has given grace, and in him I trust.
I will give him praise as I know I must.
God created me out of dirt and dust!
And my God will give me wisdom.

All God's promises are so good and true.
And he paid the price, saving me and you.
We can find his love, for it's in plain view.
And our God will give us wisdom.

God has promised us love that never dies.
And his Word won't change, for he never lies.
And the love he gives—it can make us wise!
Yes, our God will give us wisdom.

How amazing are the deeds of the LORD!
All who delight in him should ponder them. . . .
All he does is just and good,
and all his commandments are trustworthy. . . .
He has paid a full ransom for his people.
He has guaranteed his covenant with them forever.
What a holy, awe-inspiring name he has!
Fear of the LORD is the foundation of true wisdom.
All who obey his commandments will grow in wisdom.
Praise him forever!

PSALM 111:2, 7, 9-10

God Hears Me

A Psalm for When You Wonder If God Is Listening

God, you're in heaven, and you're worry free.
I am amazed at how kind you can be,
Bending way down just to listen to me!
Thank you for hearing my prayers.

Often I whisper instead of just pray.
How can you hear every word that I say?
Knowing you hear—well, it blows me away!
Thank you for hearing my prayers.

When sorrows and troubles and threats overflow,
I pray like a child who has nowhere to go.
And all of our prayers should be childlike, I know.
Thank you for hearing my prayers.

Sometimes at night when I lie on my bed,
Prayers won't come out—they just stay in my head.
But I know you hear, because that's what you said.
Thank you for hearing my prayers.

One day at school when I felt pretty sick,
Prayers filled my mind, so I sent them up quick.
Soon I was fine. That's a really cool trick!
Thank you for hearing my prayers.

What can I offer for all that you've done?
I'll give you thanks during hard times or fun.
I'll tell the world and my friends, one by one.
So thank you for hearing my prayers.

Lord, how I love you for hearing my voice!
Talking to you—that's my very best choice.
I'll listen, too; then we both can rejoice!
Thank you for hearing my prayers.

*I love the LORD because he hears
my voice and my prayer for mercy.
Because he bends down to listen,
I will pray as long as I have breath!*

PSALM 116:1-2

God Gives Me His Word

A Psalm about the Bible

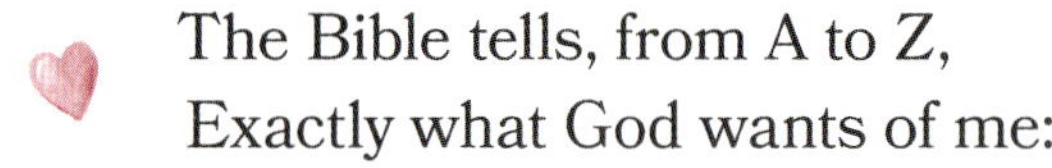

The Bible tells, from A to Z,
Exactly what God wants of me:

A **Actions** can be bad or good.
Help me live the way I should.

B **Blessings** from your Word are sure,
Guidelines that will keep me pure.

C Your **commands** are my delight,
Guiding me to do what's right.

D I **determine** to be true,
Read your Word, and cling to you.

E Give me **eyes** that open wide.
Set me free from foolish pride.

F All your words are so outstanding.
Faith will come with understanding.

G **Grace** and **goodness** come from you.
Happiness and love do too.

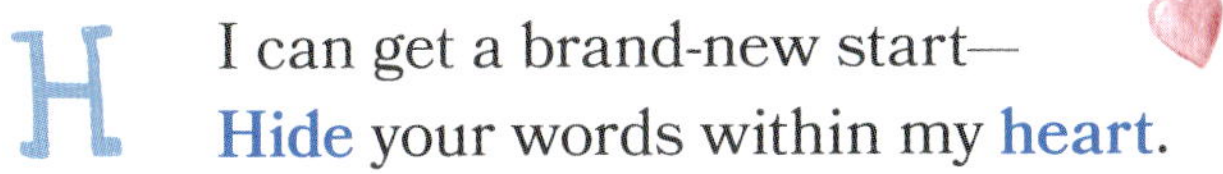

H

I can get a brand-new start—
Hide your words within my heart.

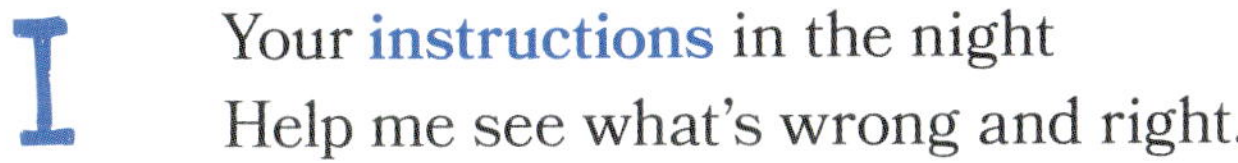

I

Your instructions in the night
Help me see what's wrong and right.

J

Justice comes when I obey.
You will always show the way.

K

Every word you give is kind,
Giving grace and peace of mind.

L

Keep me in your steady love.
True love comes from God above.

M

Just in time, before I drown,
Tender mercies tumble down.

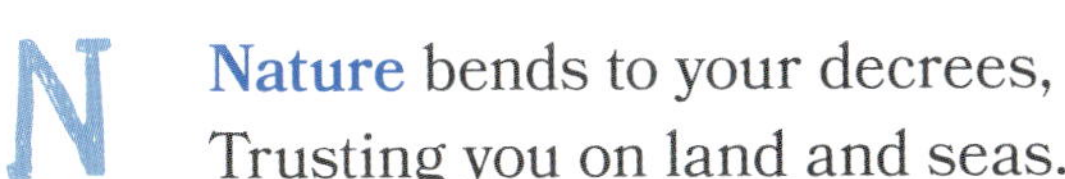

N

Nature bends to your decrees,
Trusting you on land and seas.

O

Oh, the lamp that gives me light!
I'll obey and do what's right.

P

Words of **promise**, **peace**, and **praise**—
Help me worship all my days.

Q

Quiet me with your instruction.
Keep me, Lord, from self-destruction.

R

Teach me every **regulation**—
Every word, a **revelation**!

S

Sweeter than a honeycomb,
Words will lead me home, **sweet** home.

T

In your Word your **truth** is clear.
Trusting you, I sense you're near.

U

I will memorize your Word,
Understanding what I've heard.

V

Victory is always mine.
Thanks to you, I'll rise and shine.

W

Lord, your **Word** can make me sing,
Worship you as God and King.

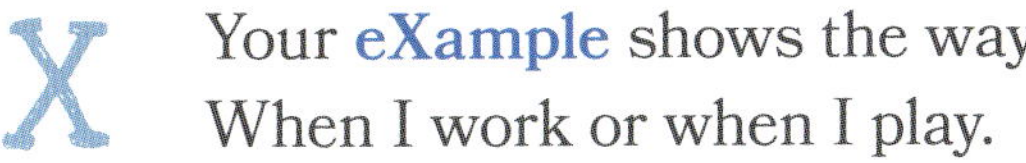

X Your **eXample** shows the way
When I work or when I play.

Y **Yes!** Your Word's a thousandfold
Better than the finest gold.

Z **Zip** my lips from speaking lies.
Only your Word satisfies.

How can a young person stay pure?
By obeying your word. . . .
I have hidden your word in my heart,
that I might not sin against you. . . .
I have rejoiced in your laws
as much as in riches.
I will study your commandments
and reflect on your ways.
I will delight in your decrees
and not forget your word. . . .
How sweet your words taste to me;
they are sweeter than honey. . . .
Truly, I love your commands
more than gold, even the finest gold.

PSALM 119:9, 11, 14-16, 103, 127

God Watches Over Me

A Psalm for When You Feel Alone

When the thunder booms and it just won't stop,
Could I give that storm a karate chop?
Should I look for help from the mountaintop?
No! God is watching over me.

If I meet some kids who are twice my size,
I could run away from those scary guys.
But I'll trust in God, for he never lies.
God is watching over me.

If a big tornado or a hurricane
Tried to run me down, I'd be right as rain.
For I'd flush my fears—send them down the drain.
God is watching over me.

If I get too hot when the sun is bright,
Or the shadows dart 'cross the moon at night,
I'll be a-okay. And you know I'm right.
God is watching over me.

When I stumble hard or I take a fall,
God will pick me up, for he sees it all.
And I'll talk to God—I know who to call.
God is watching over me.

When I'm in my bed but I'm wide awake,
If I feel alone, that's a big mistake!
I should know the truth: that for goodness' sake,
God is watching over me.

When I'm scared, my room isn't what it seems.
Then my mind plays tricks, and my ears hear screams.
But God turns my nightmares into dreams.
God is watching over me.

When I'm all grown up, when I'm old and gray,
If I live in China or the USA,
There is still one truth that you'll hear me say:
God is watching over me.

I look up to the mountains—
does my help come from there?
My help comes from the LORD,
who made heaven and earth!
He will not let you stumble; the one
who watches over you will not slumber.
Indeed, he who watches over Israel
never slumbers or sleeps. . . .
The LORD keeps watch over you as
you come and go, both now and forever.

PSALM 121:1-4, 8

God Loves Me Forever

A Psalm to Remind You That You're Loved

Thank you, God, for loving me,
Now and through eternity.
God loves me forever.

Miracles all come from you;
Every day they're in full view!
God loves me forever.

Every gift and every skill
Come to us by your good will.
God loves me forever.

Sun by day and moon by night,
Making sure we see the light.
God loves me forever.

Lord, you know I make mistakes,
Bend a rule until it breaks.
God loves me forever.

I'm so weak, and you're so strong.
You do right, and I do wrong.
God loves me forever.

Father, when I'm such a mess,
Does it make you love me less?
God loves me forever!

You have my apology.
Thank you for forgiving me.
God loves me forever!

Now I want the world to know:
Love like God's won't let me go.
God loves me forever!

Give thanks to the Lord, for he is good!
His faithful love endures forever.
Give thanks to the God of gods.
His faithful love endures forever.
Give thanks to the Lord of lords.
His faithful love endures forever.

PSALM 136:1-3

God Is Always with Me

A Psalm for When You Want to Be Known

If I climb, climb, climb up the tallest tree,
Even way up high, God is watching me.

If I swim down, down in the ocean blue,
Deep as I can go, God is down there too.

If I find a cave and I hide in there,
I can't hide from God. God is everywhere!

If I run away, far as I can go,
I won't run from God. God will always know.

If a storm kicks up and the lights go out,
God can hear my prayer. I won't need to shout.

When I'm on my bike and I take a fall,
God will pick me up, 'cause he sees it all.

If I'm at my friend's on an overnight,
God is right there too—he's just out of sight.

If I have to switch to a school that's new,
I won't be alone. God will go there too!

I don't like it much when I'm last in line.
But since God's there too, guess I'll be just fine.

If I'm in the car on a boring ride,
God can share my seat. He'll be by my side.

If I sailed to earth in a parachute,
God would come along, just to troubleshoot.

If I went to Mars at the speed of light,
God would go there too, for the long, long flight.

God goes everywhere I could ever go!
And I'll tell you why . . . 'cause he loves me so!

I can never escape from your Spirit!
I can never get away from your presence!
If I go up to heaven, you are there;
if I go down to the grave, you are there.
If I ride the wings of the morning,
if I dwell by the farthest oceans,
even there your hand will guide me,
and your strength will support me.
I could ask the darkness to hide me
and the light around me to become night—
but even in darkness I cannot hide from you.
To you the night shines as bright as day.
Darkness and light are the same to you.

PSALM 139:7-12

God Listens

A Psalm for When You Need Hope

Here in the dark, I am losing all hope,
Wondering whether or not I can cope,
Frightened that I'm at the end of my rope.
Lord, will you please hear my prayer?

Nobody likes me. I feel so alone.
Stumbling and falling, I'm accident prone.
Wish I could reach you by calling your phone.
Lord, will you please hear my prayer?

Even my very best friend told a lie.
His new best friend is a not-so-nice guy.
I am left out, and I wish I knew why.
Lord, will you please hear my prayer?

I can remember, not that long ago,
All of my sins were washed whiter than snow.
Now I can't find you—I look high and low.
Lord, will you please hear my prayer?

I'm very thirsty, Lord—thirsty for you.
Yearning for faith and the peace I once knew.
Tell me, dear God, what on earth should I do?
Lord, will you please hear my prayer?

Rescue me, Father! I'm helpless and weak.
You are my life, and it's you that I seek.
I'm just your servant. I'll hear when you speak.
Lord, will you please hear my prayer?

Thinking of all the great things you have done—
Love comes each morning, brand new, like the sun—
I could keep counting your gifts, one by one.
Surely you're hearing my prayers.

I am your servant; please show me the way.
Give me your strength so I won't disobey.
Father, you hear every word that I say.
Thank you for hearing my prayers!

Hear my prayer, O Lord;
listen to my plea!
Answer me because you are faithful and righteous. . . .
I remember the days of old.
I ponder all your great works
and think about what you have done.
I lift my hands to you in prayer.
I thirst for you as parched land thirsts for rain. . . .
Let me hear of your unfailing love each morning,
for I am trusting you.
Show me where to walk,
for I give myself to you.

PSALM 143:1, 5-6, 8

God Takes Care of Me

A Psalm for When You Need Someone on Your Side

I would like to say: you're my God and King.
You're my Lord, Creator of everything!
It's to you I pray; it's to you I sing!
Father, you take care of me.

When a lion deep in the jungle roars,
He needs food to eat in the great outdoors.
And he's so content that at night he snores,
Dreaming, "God takes care of me."

A giraffe needs leaves from a tree or two,
And a calf needs milk when it's just brand new.
They will both be fine and give thanks to you:
Saying, "God takes care of us!"

When I feed my horse from a bale of hay,
Then my horse responds with a friendly neigh.
But hay comes from YOU, so my horse should say:
"Lord God, you take care of me."

You're a mighty king! Yet you always care.
When I'm feeling sad, I know you'll be there.
And I see your love, 'cause it's everywhere!
I know you take care of me.

Lord, you don't get mad when I don't obey.
You forgive my sins, and you're here to stay.
It's so great that you love me anyway
And that you take care of me.

Since you pick me up when I fall behind,
I will tell the world that you're strong and kind.
Lord, the way you care really blows my mind!
Father, you take care of me.

Every living thing shouts with hip-hoorays.
We will all give thanks! We will all give praise!
And I know for sure that for all my days . . .
Father, you take care of me.

The LORD is merciful and compassionate,
slow to get angry and filled with unfailing love.
The LORD is good to everyone.
He showers compassion on all his creation. . . .
The eyes of all look to you in hope;
you give them their food as they need it.
When you open your hand,
you satisfy the hunger and thirst
of every living thing.

PSALM 145:8-9, 15-16

About the Author

DANDI DALEY MACKALL is the award-winning author of about 500 books for children and adults. She visits countless schools, conducts writing assemblies and workshops across the United States, and presents keynote addresses at conferences and events for young authors. She is also a frequent guest on radio talk shows and has made dozens of appearances on TV. She has won several awards for her writing, including the Helen Keating Ott Award for Outstanding Contribution to Children's Literature and the Edgar Award, and is a two-time winner of the Christian Book Award and the Mom's Choice Award.

Dandi writes from rural Ohio, where she lives with her husband, surrounded by their three children, four granddaughters, and a host of animals. Visit her at DandiBooks.com and www.facebook.com/dandi.mackall.